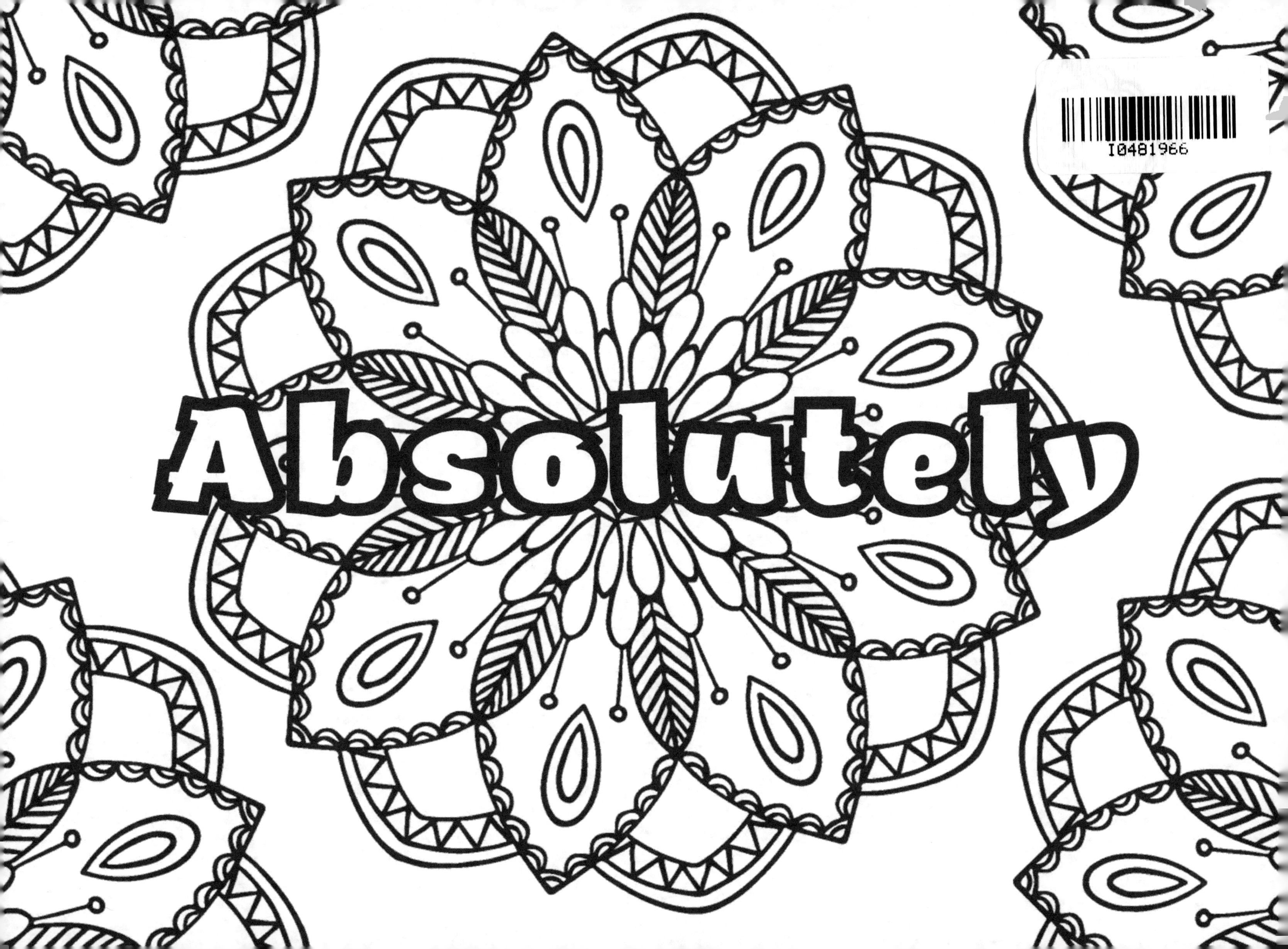
Absolutely

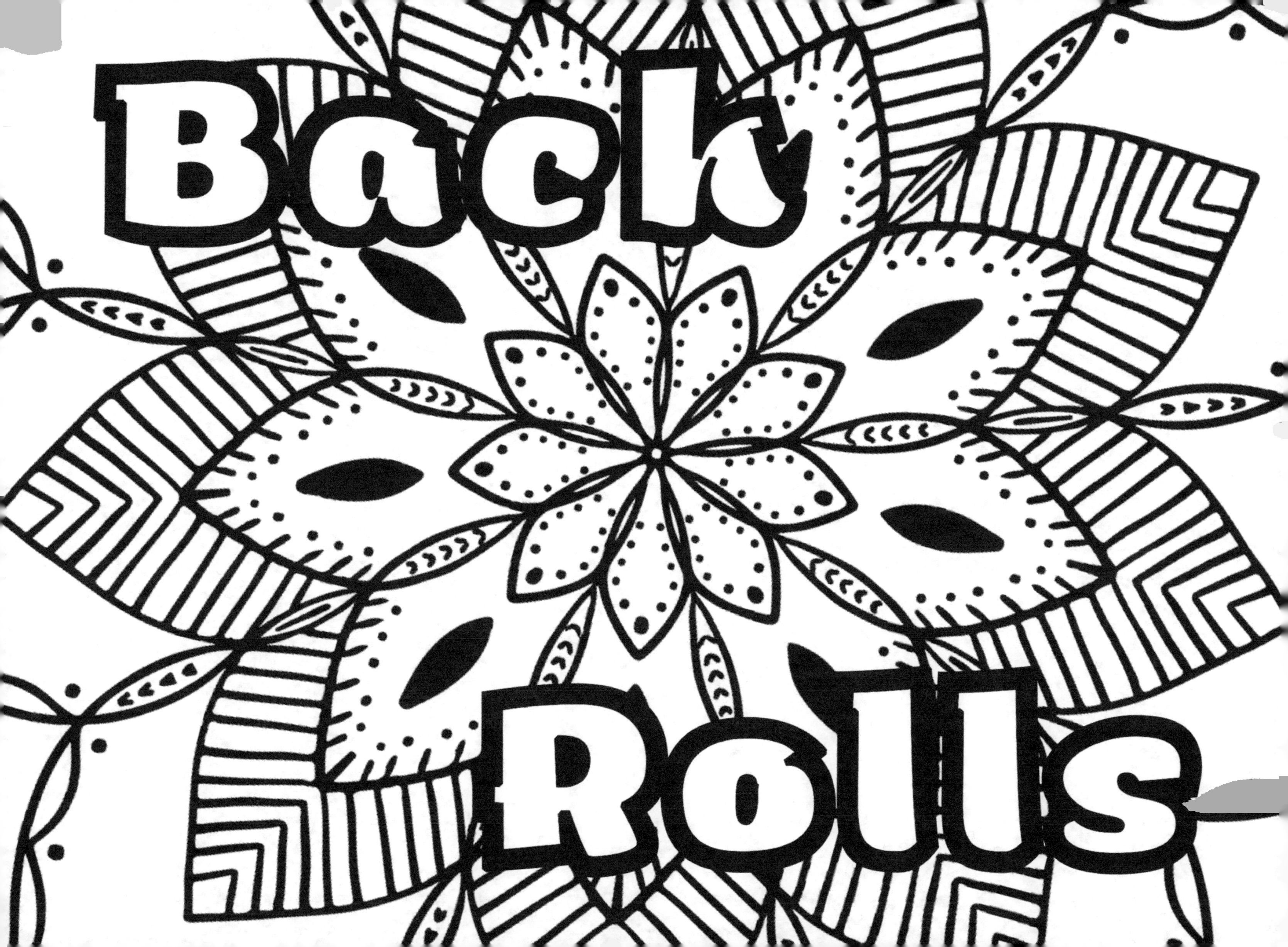
Back
Rolls

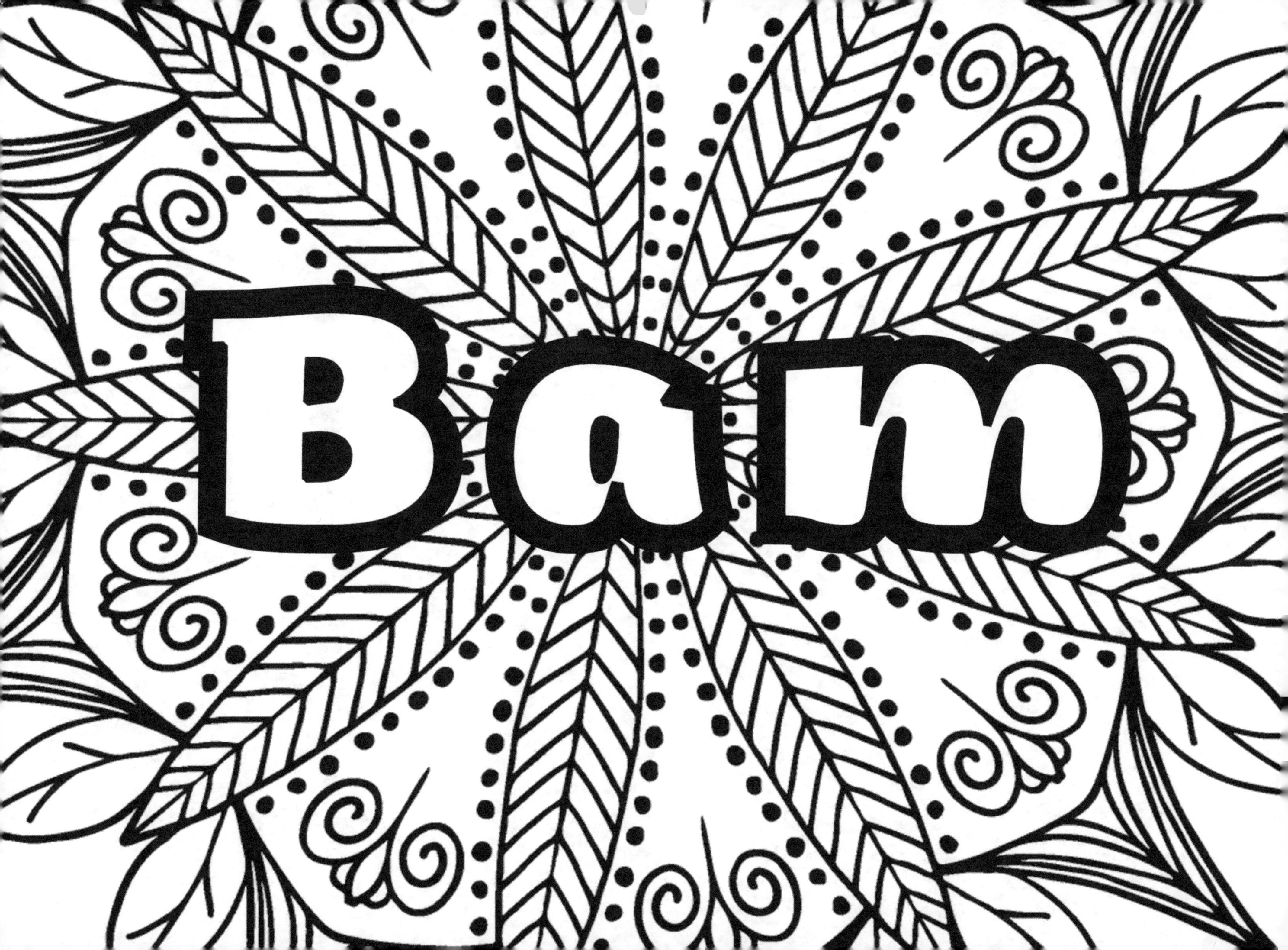
Bam

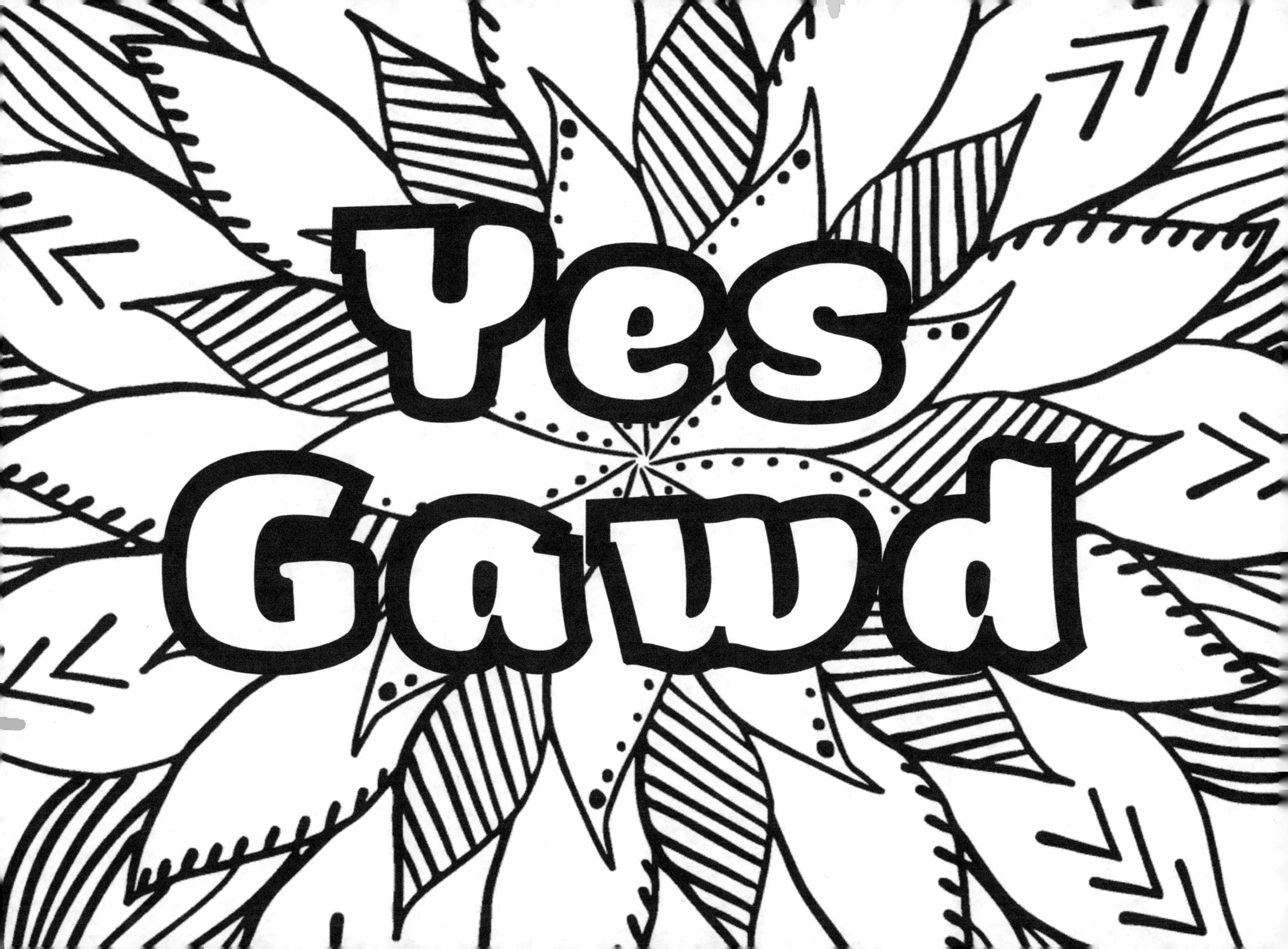
Yes
Gawd

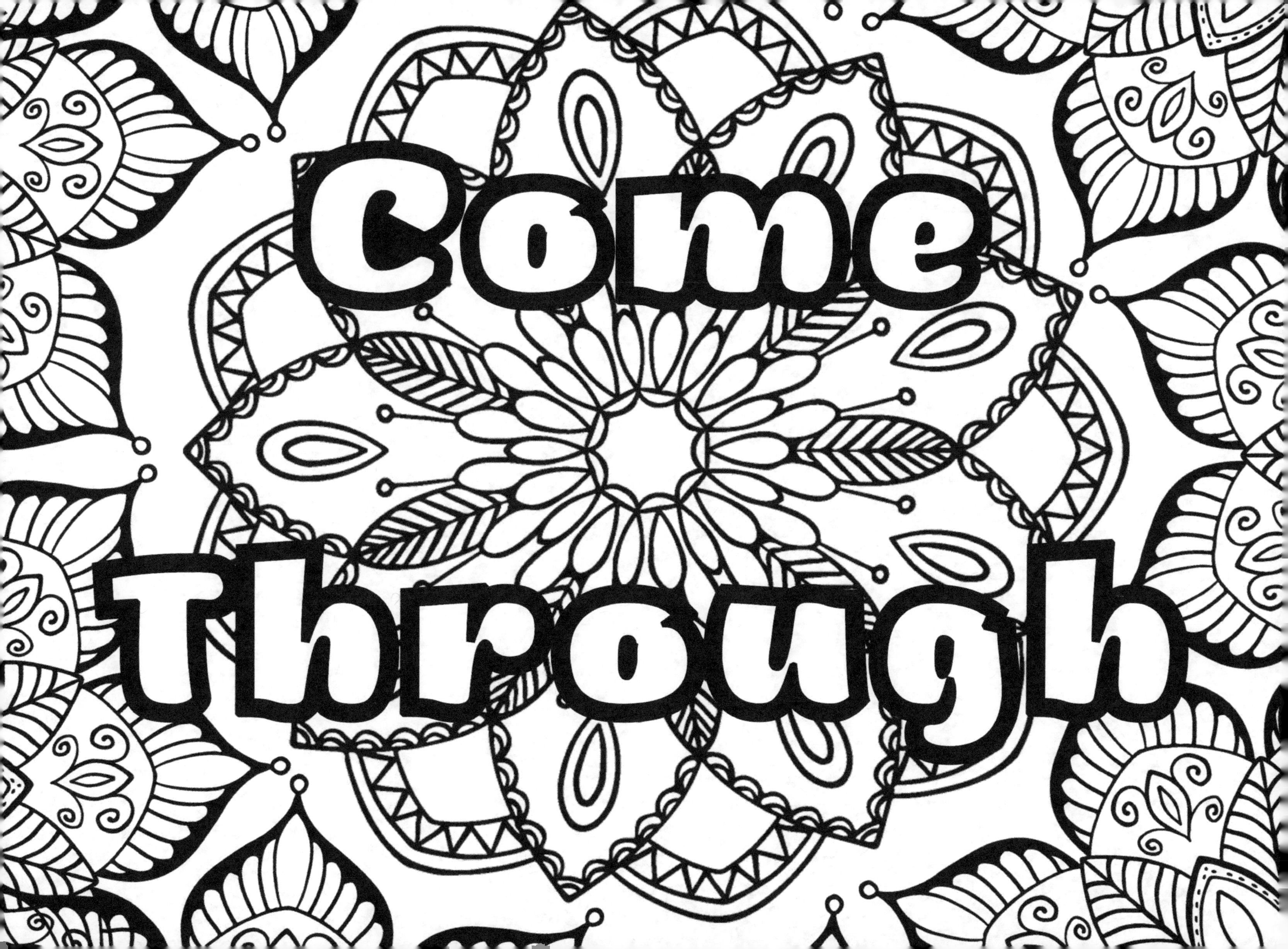
Come
Through

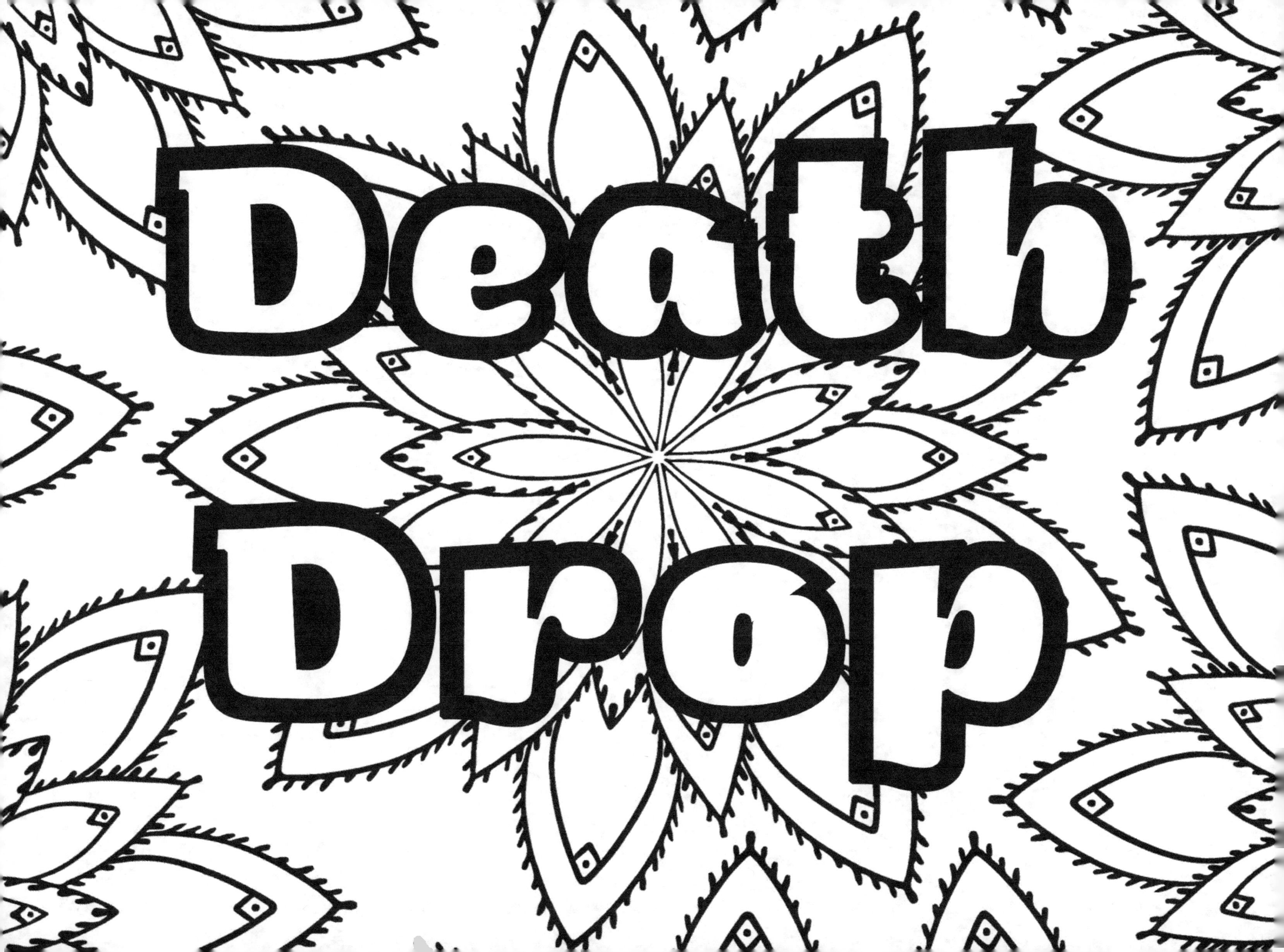
Death
Drop

I don't
get cute
I get
drop dead
GORGEOUS

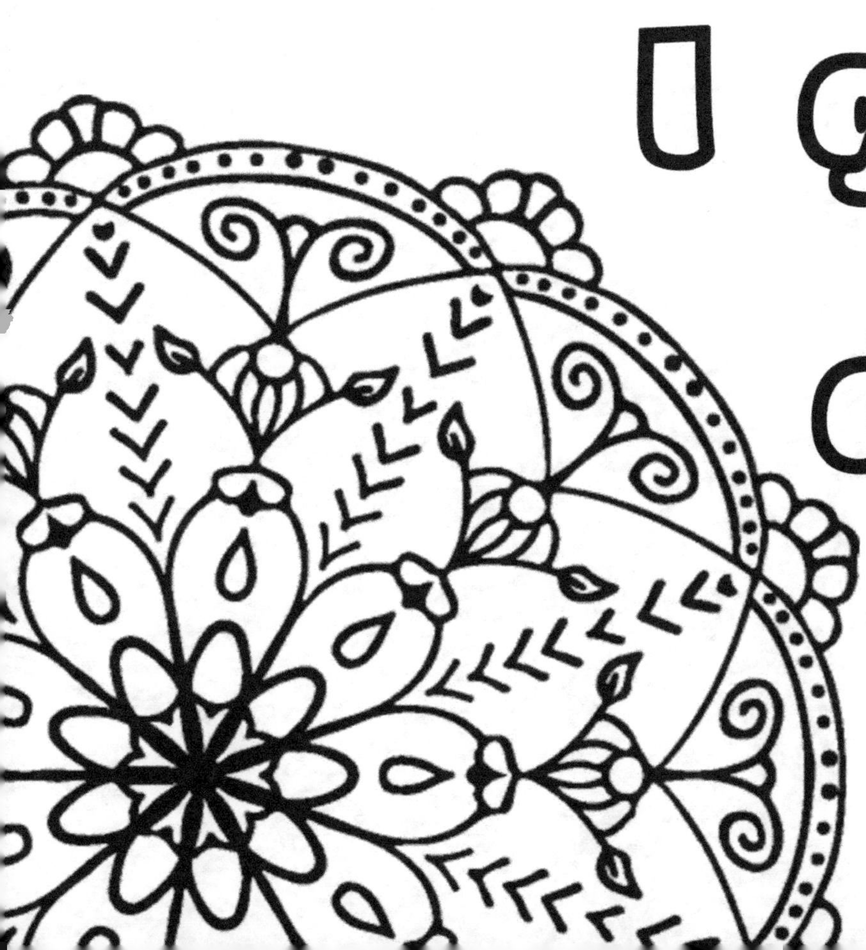

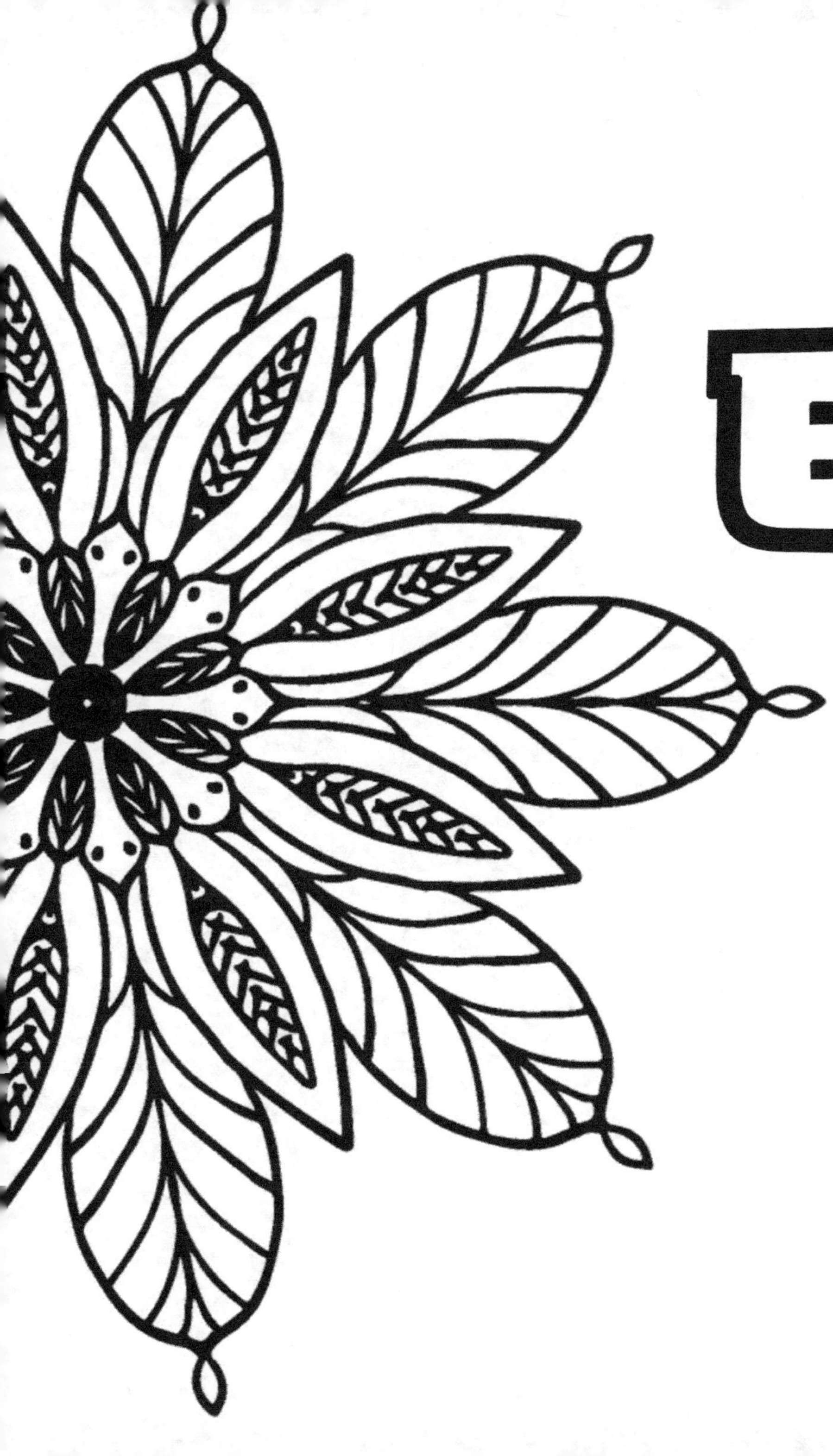

Eat It

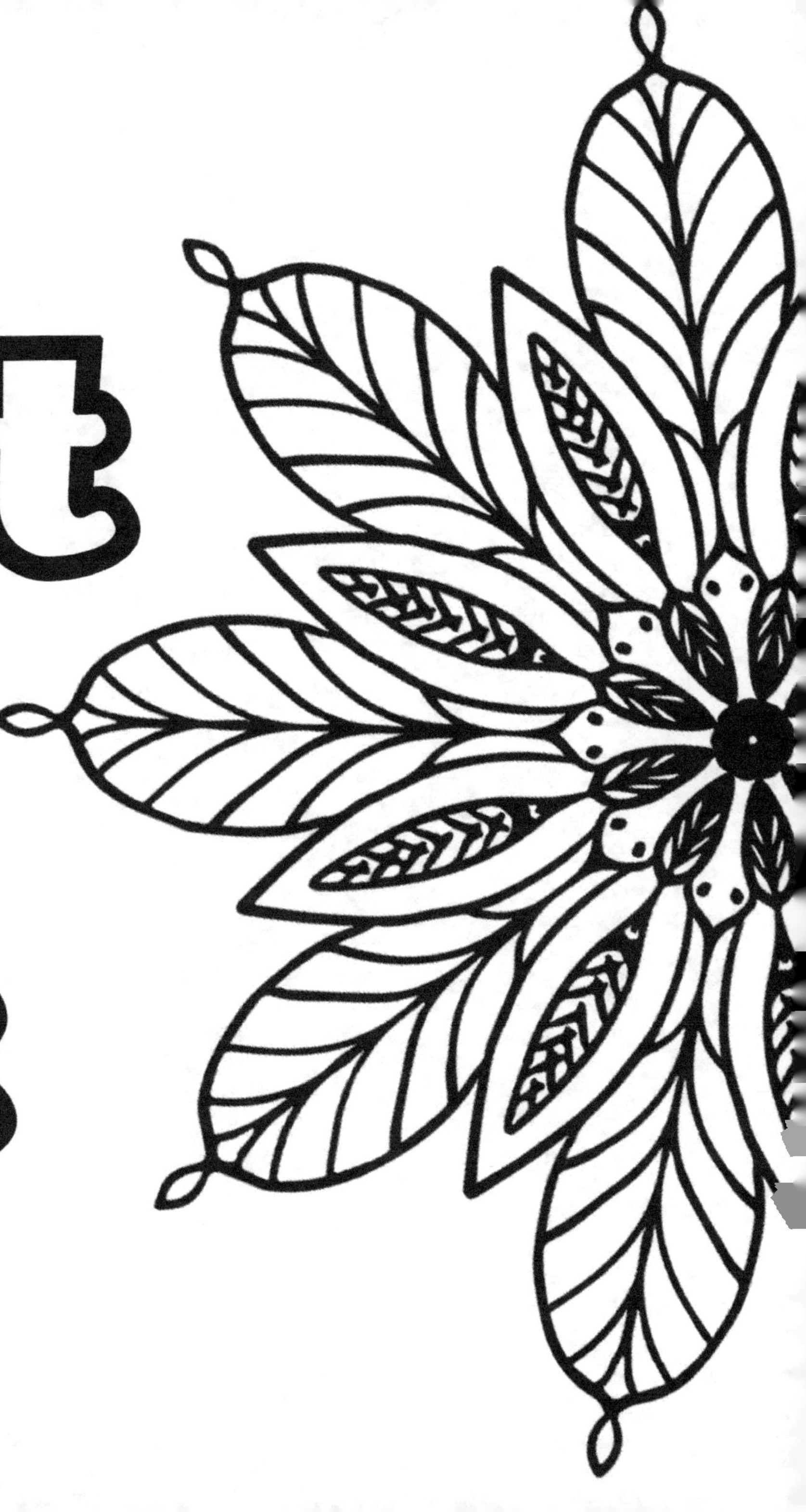

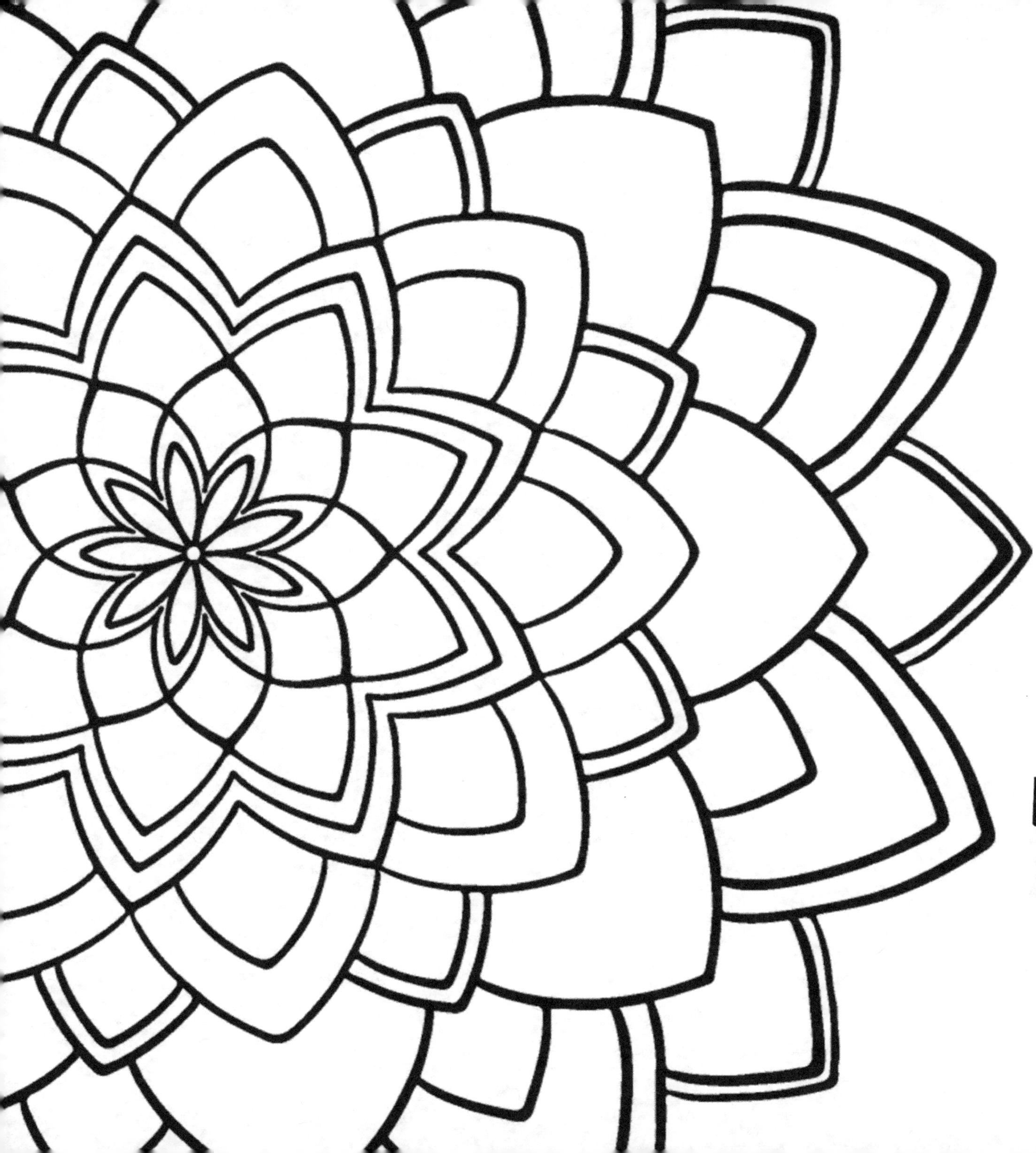

Fla Say Dah

Halleloo

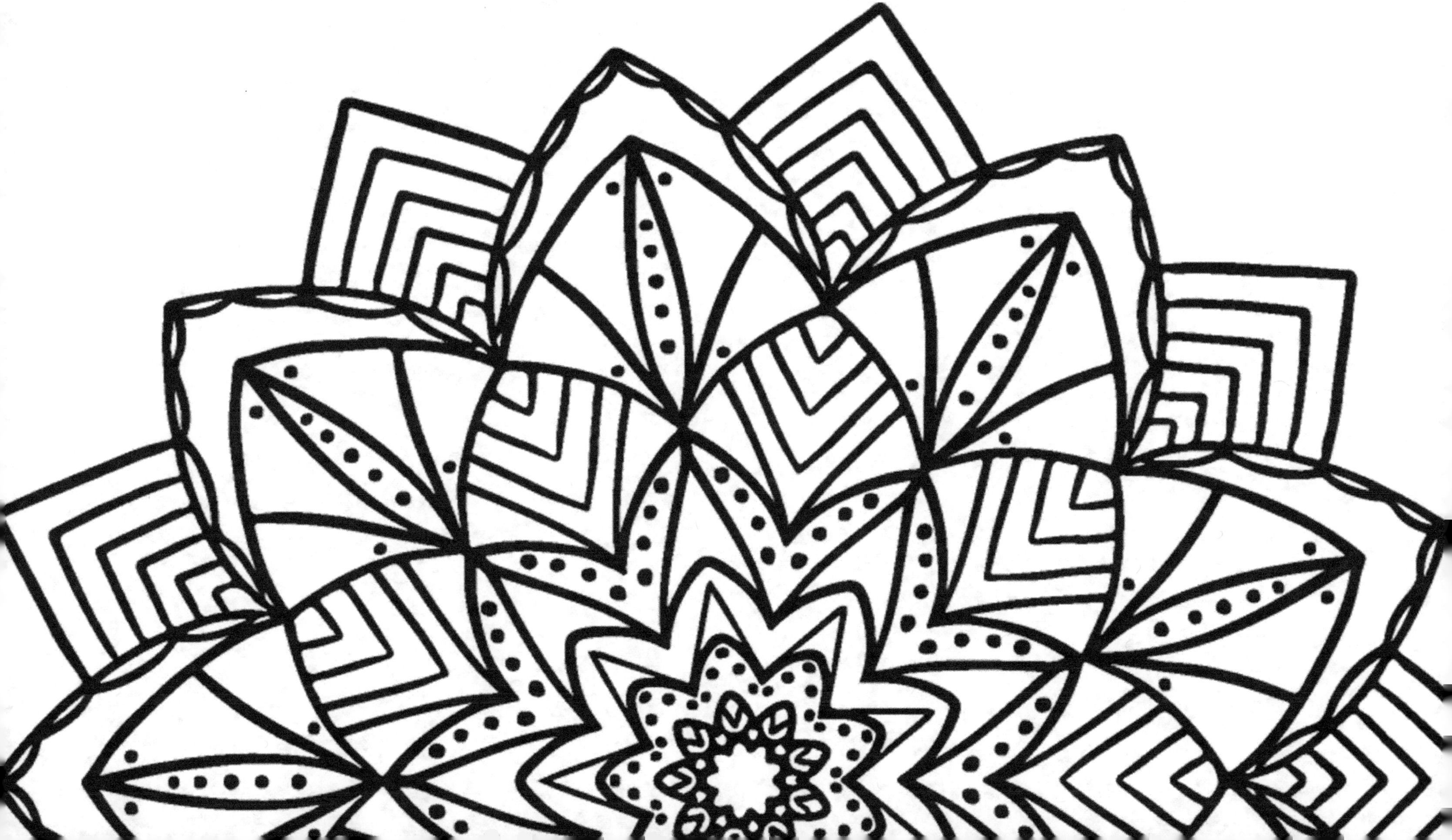

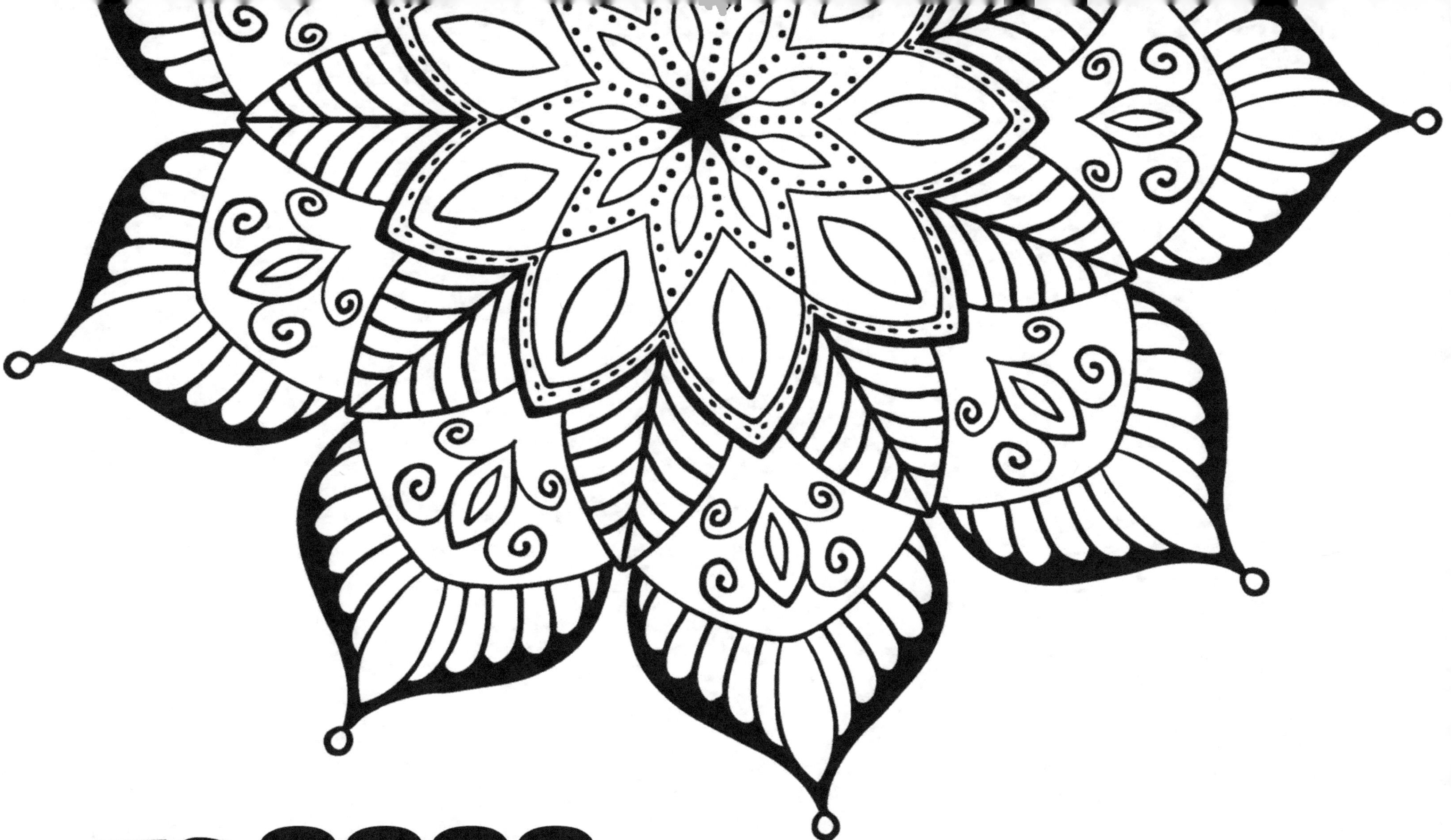

Hiiiieeeeee

The Library is open

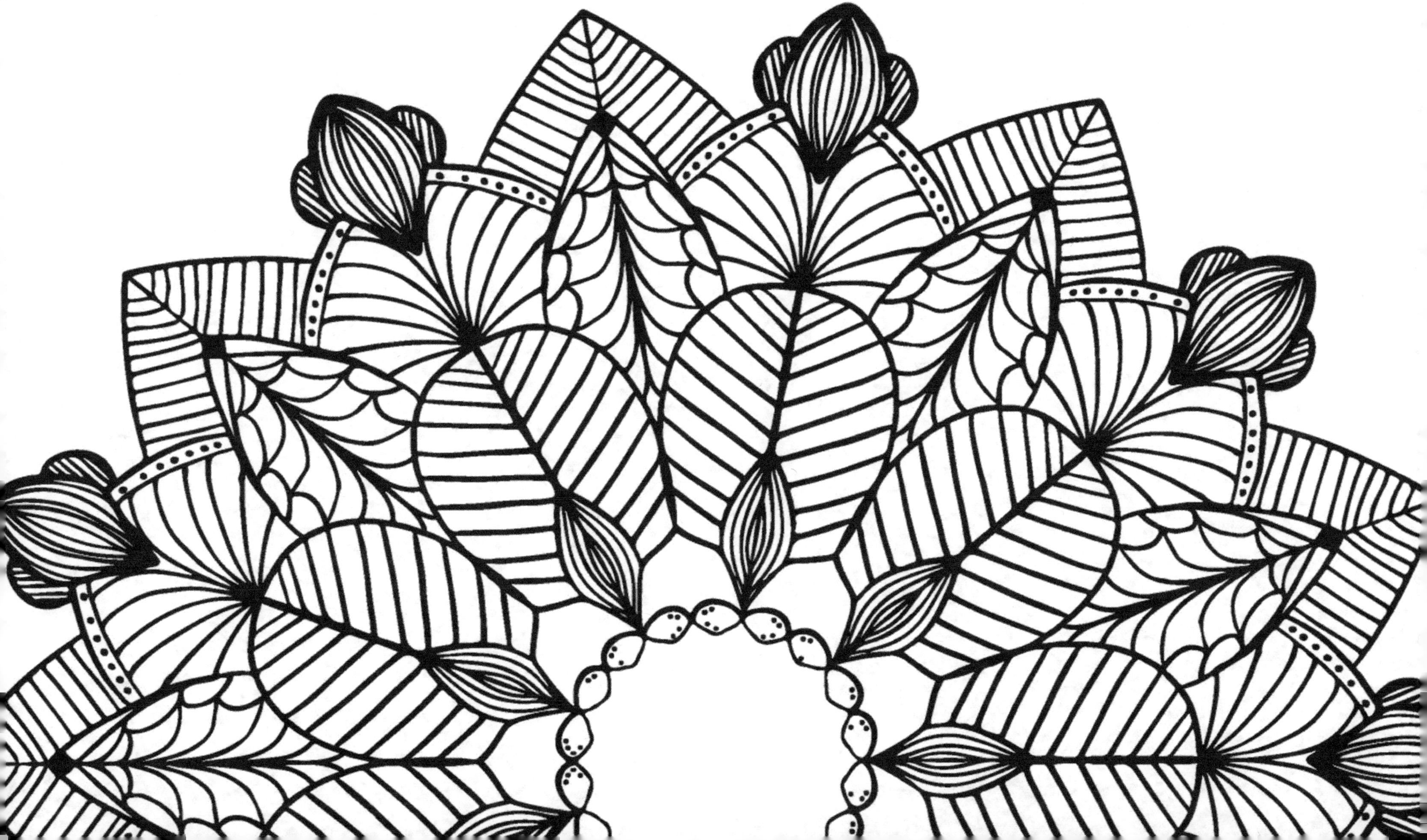

Miss Vanjie

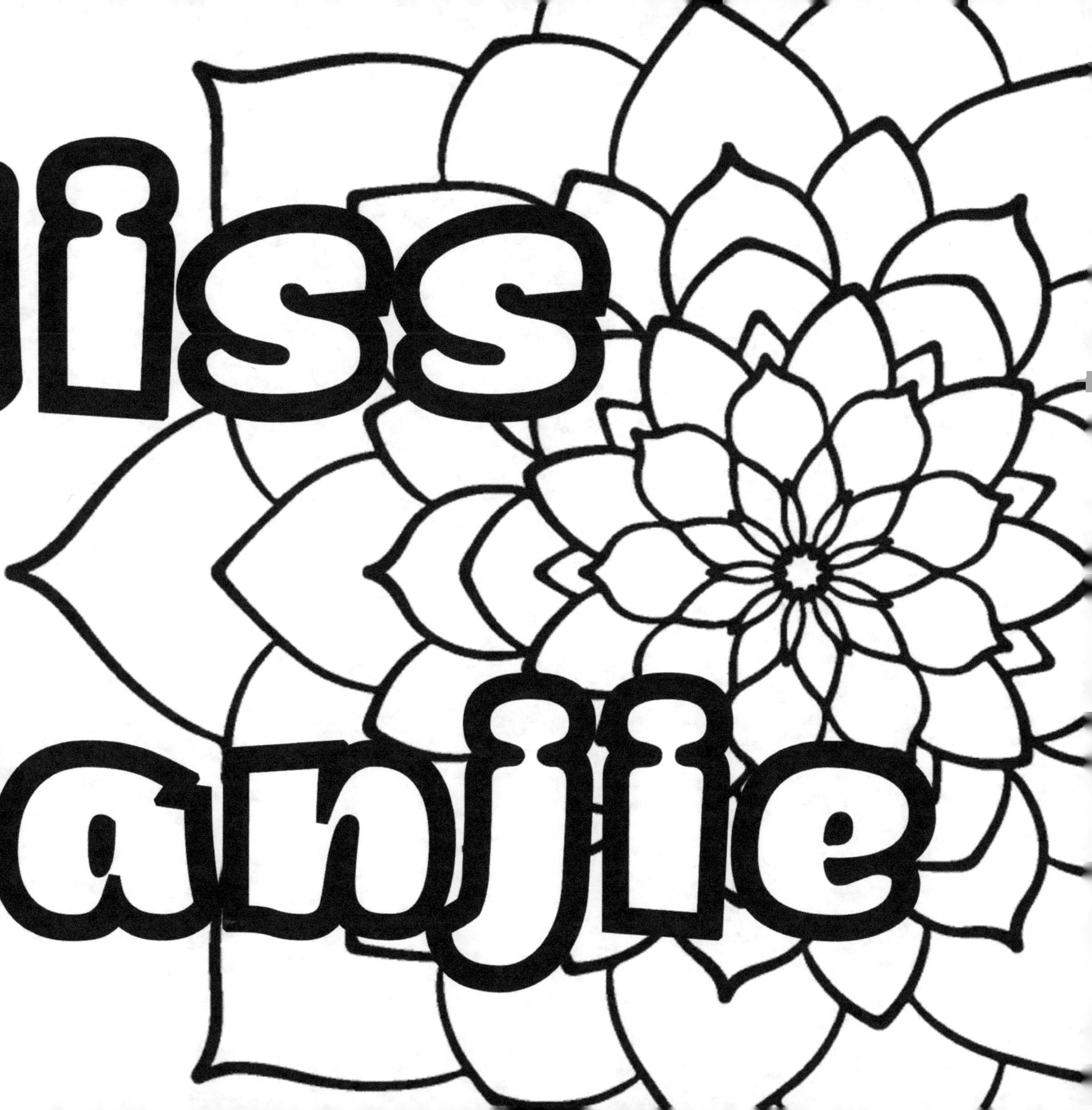

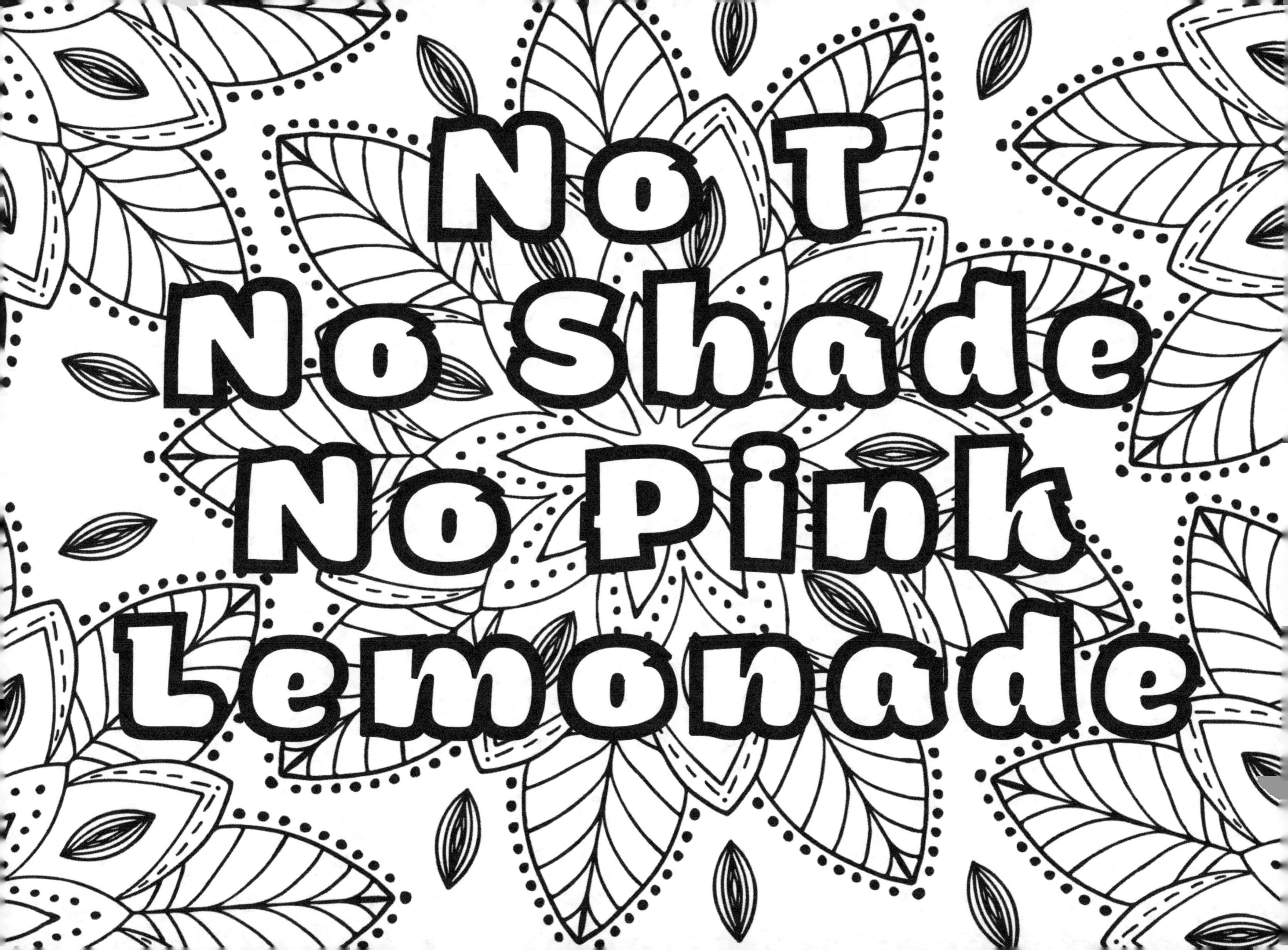
No T
No Shade
No Pink
Lemonade

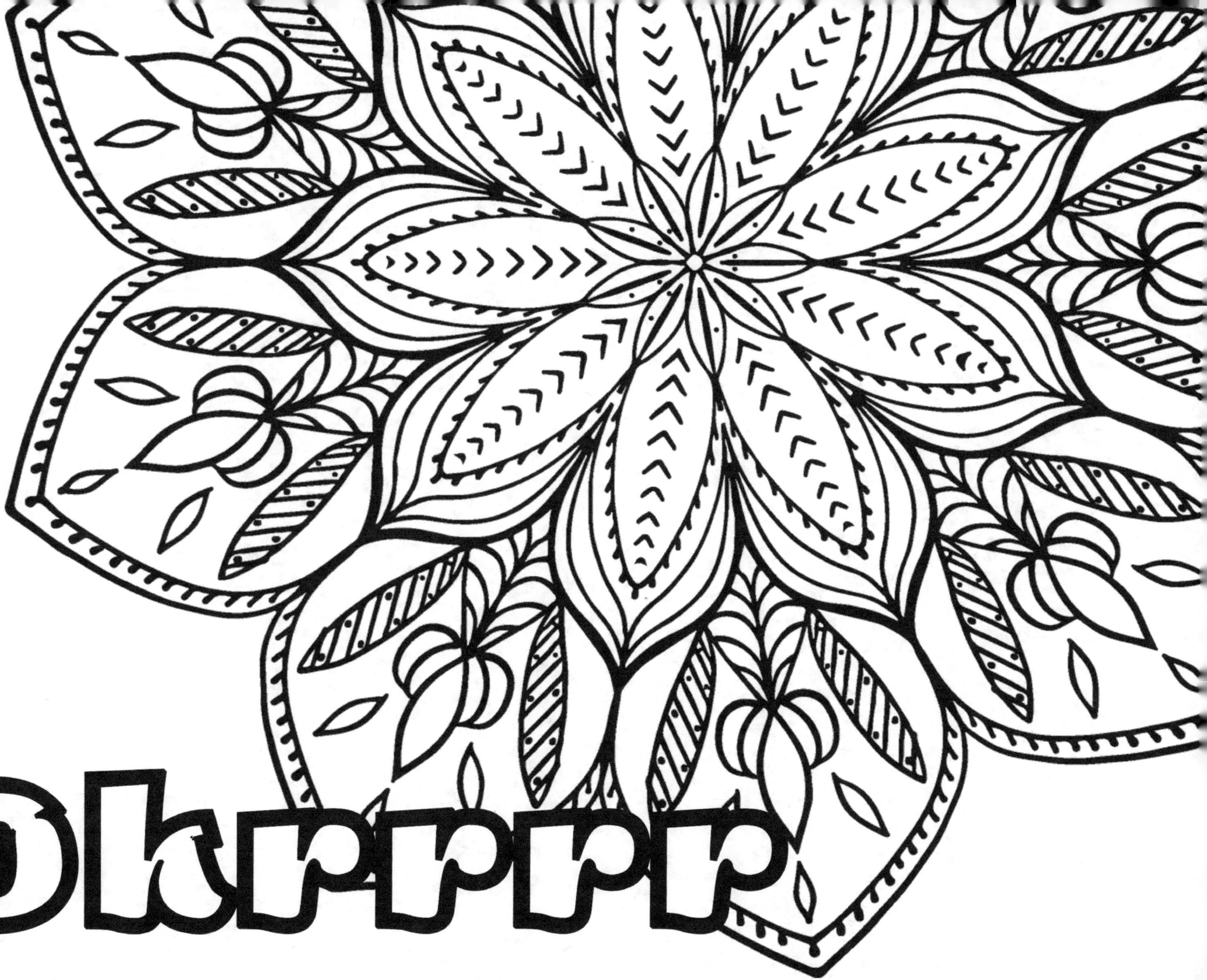

Okrrrr

Party

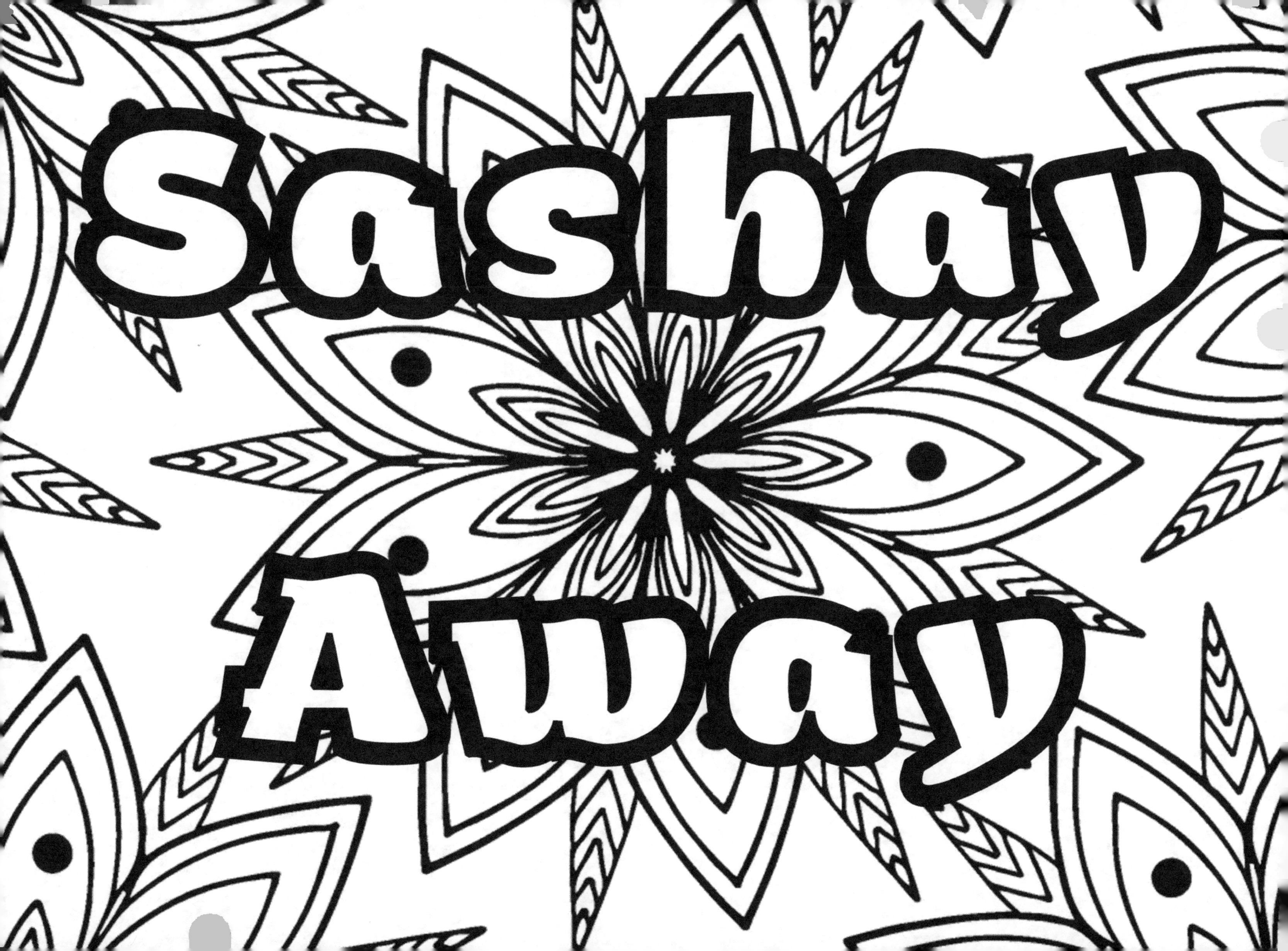
Sashay
Away

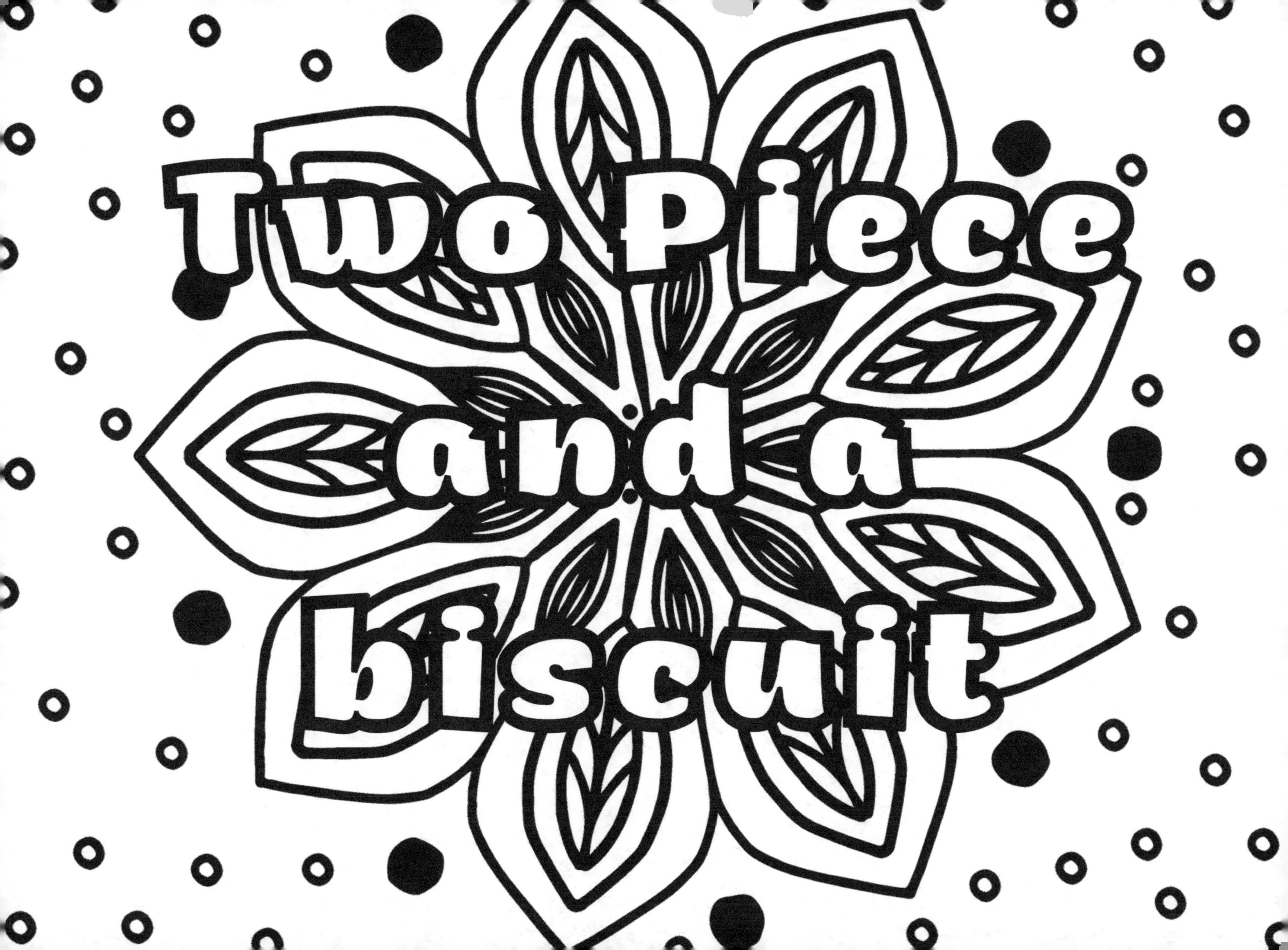
Two Piece
and a
biscuit

Water off a duck's back

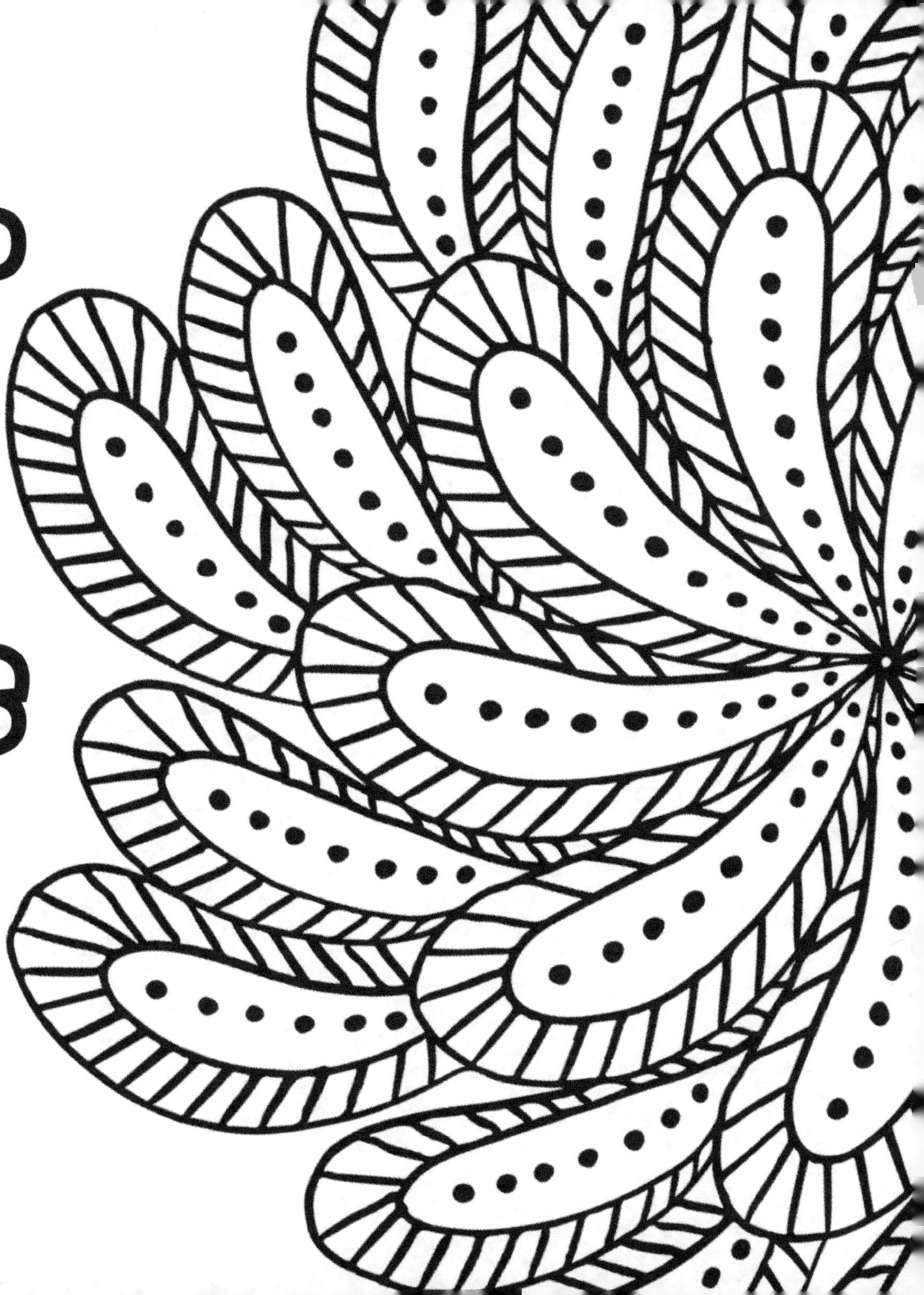

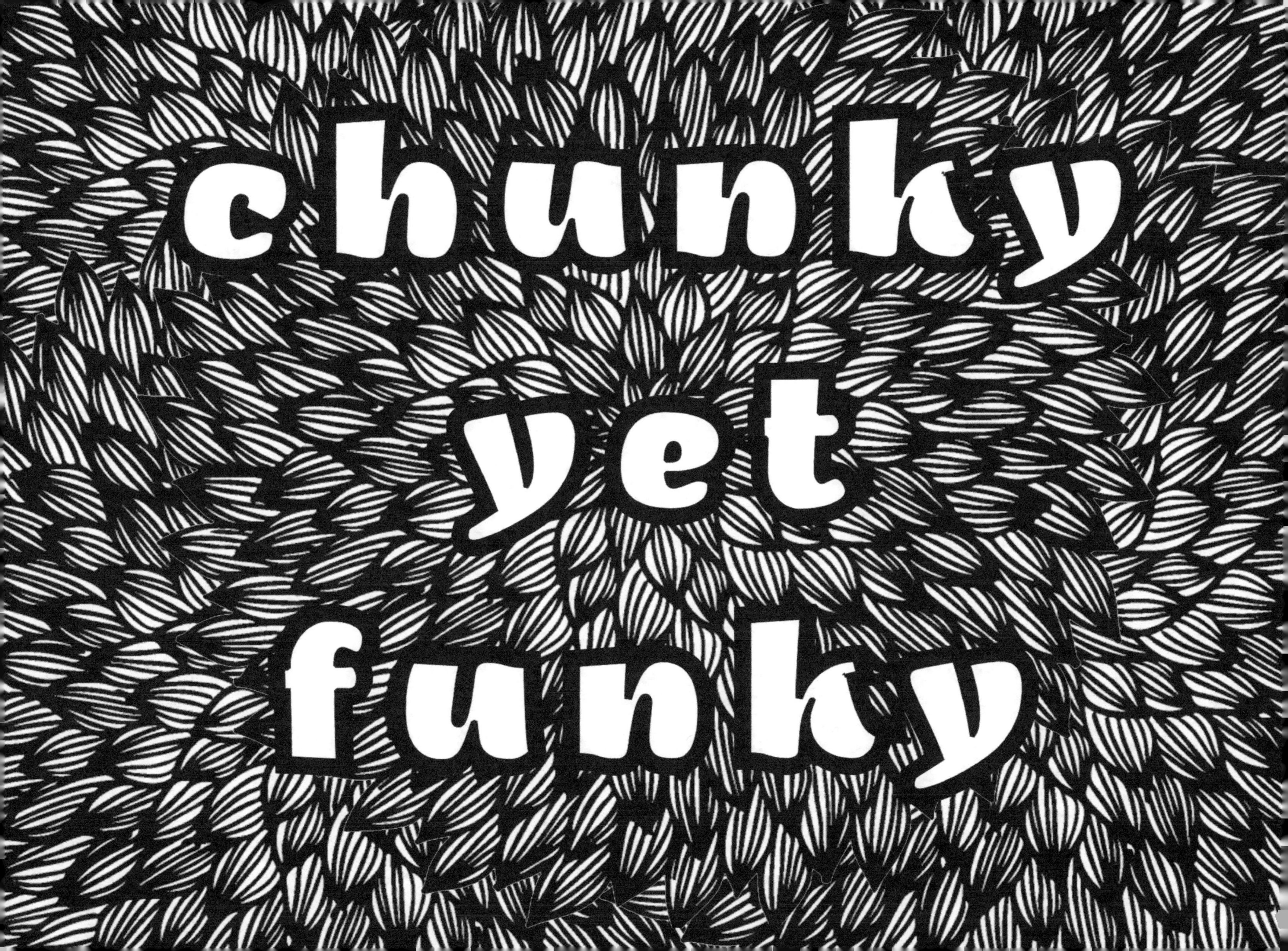
chunky
yet
funky

www.ingramcontent.com/pod-product-compliance
Lightning Source LLC
Chambersburg PA
CBHW080139240526
45468CB00009BA/2583
* 9 7 8 1 7 2 2 1 2 4 8 8 5 *